JAN 30 2003   **DATE DUE**

Demco, Inc. 38-293

SandCastle 3

Homonyms

Do Not Squash the Squash

Kelly Doudna

ABDO
Publishing Company

Published by SandCastle™, an imprint of ABDO Publishing Company, 4940 Viking Drive, Edina, Minnesota 55435.

Printed in the United States.

Photo credits: Corbis Images, Digital Vision, Eyewire Images, PhotoDisc, PictureQuest

Library of Congress Cataloging-in-Publication Data

Doudna, Kelly, 1963-
    Do not squash the squash / Kelly Doudna.
        p. cm. -- (Homonyms)
    Includes index.
    Summary: Photographs and simple text introduce homonyms, words that are spelled and sound the same but have different meanings.
        ISBN 1-57765-791-8
        1. English language--Homonyms--Juvenile literature. [1. English language--Homonyms.] I. Title.

PE1595 .D69 2002
428.1--dc21

2001053322

The SandCastle concept, content, and reading method have been reviewed and approved by a national advisory board including literacy specialists, librarians, elementary school teachers, early childhood education professionals, and parents.

Let Us Know

After reading the book, SandCastle would like you to tell us your stories about reading. What is your favorite page? Was there something hard that you needed help with? Share the ups and downs of learning to read. We want to hear from you! To get posted on the Abdo Publishing Company Web site, send us email at:

sandcastle@abdopub.com

About SandCastle™

Nonfiction books for the beginning reader

- Basic concepts of phonics are incorporated with integrated language methods of reading instruction. Most words are short, and phrases, letter sounds, and word sounds are repeated.

- Book levels are based on the ATOS™ for Books formula. Other considerations for readability include the number of words in each sentence, the number of characters in each word, and word lists based on curriculum frameworks.

- Full-color photography reinforces word meanings and concepts.

- "Words I Can Read" list at the end of each book teaches basic elements of grammar, helps the reader recognize the words in the text, and builds vocabulary.

- Reading levels are indicated by the number of flags on the castle.

SandCastle uses the following definitions for this series:

- Homographs: words that are spelled the same but sound different and have different meanings. *Easy memory tip: "-graph"= same look*

- Homonyms: words that are spelled and sound the same but have different meanings. *Easy memory tip: "-nym"= same name*

- Homophones: words that sound alike but are spelled differently and have different meanings. *Easy memory tip: "-phone"= sound alike*

Look for more SandCastle books in these three reading levels:

Level 1 (one flag)	**Level 2** (two flags)	**Level 3** (three flags)

Grades Pre-K to K 5 or fewer words per page	**Grades K to 1** 5 to 10 words per page	**Grades 1 to 2** 10 to 15 words per page

star

star

Homonyms are words that are
spelled and sound the same but
have different meanings.

Dad builds houses.

He uses a saw to cut wood.

I looked around.

I saw pretty flowers in the garden.

I ride the bus to school every day.

My friends also ride it.

There are a lot of fish.

A group of fish swimming together is a school.

This baby seal lies in the snow.

It has thick fur to keep it warm.

I wrote a letter.

I will seal the envelope before I mail it.

I love watermelon.

When I finish this piece I will have seconds.

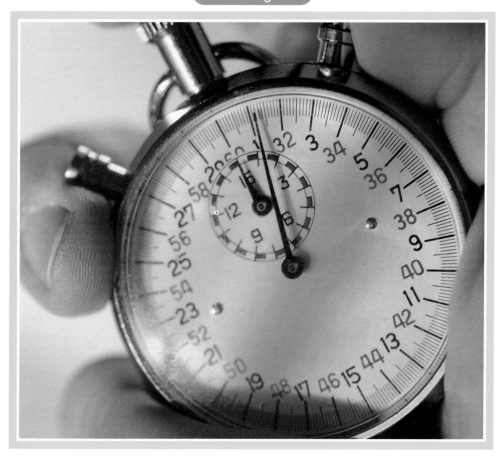

Clocks and watches help us keep time.

One minute is made up of sixty
seconds.

My dog and I were playing.

We will lie here and rest for a spell.

I like school.

Every day I learn how to spell more words.

I found a shell at the beach.

I stoop to pick it up.

I sit on the front stoop while I wait for Mom.

My kitten has soft fur.

She purrs when I stroke her.

I use the paintbrush to make a gray
stroke on the paper.

I want to stay outside.

I will sit here and stall for time.

This horse lives in a barn.

What does he look out of?

(stall)

Words I Can Read

Nouns

A noun is a person, place, or thing

barn (BARN) p. 21
beach (BEECH) p. 16
bus (BUHSS) p. 8
clocks (KLOKSS) p. 13
day (DAY) pp. 8, 15
dog (DAWG) p. 14
envelope
  (EN-vuh-lope) p. 11
fish (FISH) p. 9
flowers (FLOU-urz) p. 7
friends (FRENDZ) p. 8
fur (FUR) pp. 10, 18
garden (GARD-uhn)
  p. 7
group (GROOP) p. 9
homonyms
  (HOM-uh-nimz) p. 5

horse (HORSS) p. 21
houses (HOUSS-ez) p. 6
kitten (KIT-uhn) p. 18
letter (LET-ur) p. 11
lot (LOT) p. 9
meanings (MEE-ningz)
  p. 5
minute (MIN-it) p. 13
paintbrush
  (PAYNT-bruhsh) p. 19
paper (PAY-pur) p. 19
piece (PEESS) p. 12
saw (SAW) p. 6
school (SKOOL)
  pp. 8, 9, 15
seal (SEEL) p. 10
seconds (SEK-uhndz)
  pp. 12, 13

shell (SHEL) p. 16
snow (SNOH) p. 10
spell (SPEL) p. 14
stall (STAWL) p. 21
star (STAR) p. 4
stoop (STOOP) p. 17
stroke (STROHK) p. 19
time (TIME) pp. 13, 20
watches (WOCH-ez)
  p. 13
watermelon
  (WAW-tur-mel-uhn)
  p. 12
wood (WUD) p. 6
words (WURDZ)
  pp. 5, 15

Proper Nouns

A proper noun is the name of a
person, place, or thing

Dad (DAD) p. 6   Mom (MOM) p. 17

Pronouns

A pronoun is a word that replaces a noun

he (HEE) pp. 6, 21
her (HUR) p. 18
I (EYE) pp. 7, 8, 11, 12, 14, 15, 16, 17, 18, 19, 20

it (IT) pp. 8, 10, 11, 16
she (SHEE) p. 18
that (THAT) p. 5
there (THAIR) p. 9

us (UHSS) p. 13
we (WEE) p. 14
what (WUHT) p. 21

Verbs

A verb is an action or being word

are (AR) pp. 5, 9
builds (BILDZ) p. 6
cut (KUHT) p. 6
does (DUHZ) p. 21
finish (FIN-ish) p. 12
found (FOUND) p. 16
has (HAZ) pp. 10, 18
have (HAV) pp. 5, 12
help (HELP) p. 13
is (IZ) pp. 9, 13
keep (KEEP) pp. 10, 13
learn (LURN) p. 15
lie (LYE) p. 14
lies (LYEZ) p. 10
like (LIKE) p. 15
lives (LIVZ) p. 21

look (LUK) p. 21
looked (LUKT) p. 7
love (LUHV) p. 12
made (MAYD) p. 13
mail (MAYL) p. 11
make (MAYK) p. 19
pick (PIK) p. 16
playing (PLAY-ing) p. 14
purrs (PURZ) p. 18
rest (REST) p. 14
ride (RIDE) p. 8
saw (SAW) p. 7
seal (SEEL) p. 11
sit (SIT) pp. 17, 20
sound (SOUND) p. 5
spell (SPEL) p. 15

spelled (SPELD) p. 5
stall (STAWL) p. 20
stay (STAY) p. 20
stoop (STOOP) p. 16
stroke (STROHK) p. 18
swimming (SWIM-ing) p. 9
use (YOOZ) p. 19
uses (YOOZ-ez) p. 6
wait (WATE) p. 17
want (WONT) p. 20
were (WUR) p. 14
will (WIL) pp. 11, 12, 14, 20
wrote (ROTE) p. 11

Adjectives

An adjective describes something

baby (BAY-bee) p. 10
different (DIF-ur-uhnt)
  p. 5
every (EV-ree) pp. 8, 15
front (FRUHNT) p. 17
gray (GRAY) p. 19

more (MOR) p. 15
my (MYE) pp. 8, 14, 18
one (WUHN) p. 13
pretty (PRIT-ee) p. 7
same (SAYM) p. 5
sixty (SIKS-tee) p. 13

soft (SAWFT) p. 18
thick (THIK) p. 10
this (THISS)
  pp. 10, 12, 21
up (UHP) p. 16
warm (WORM) p. 10

Adverbs

An adverb tells how, when, or where something happens

also (AWL-soh) p. 8
around (uh-ROUND)
  p. 7

here (HIHR) pp. 14, 20
outside (out-SIDE) p. 20

together
  (tuh-GETH-ur) p. 9
up (UHP) p. 13